Priesthood and Ministry

The Lutheran Difference Series

William M. Cwirla

CONCORDIA PUBLISHING HOUSE • SAINT LOUIS

Copyright © 2007 by Concordia Publishing House
3558 S. Jefferson Ave.
St. Louis, MO 63118-3968
1-800-325-3040 • www.cph.org

All rights reserved. No part of this publication may be reproduced, stored in a retrieval system, or transmitted, in any form or by any means, electronic, mechanical, photocopying, recording, or otherwise, without the prior written permission of Concordia Publishing House.

Written by William M. Cwirla

Edited by Robert C. Baker

Scripture quotations are from The Holy Bible, English Standard Version ®. Copyright © 2001 by Crossway Bibles, a publishing ministry of Good News Publishers, Wheaton, Illinois. Used by permission. All rights reserved.

The quotations from the Lutheran Confessions in this publication are from *Concordia: The Lutheran Confessions*, second edition, copyright © 2006 Concordia Publishing House. All rights reserved.

The quotations from Luther's Works in this publication are from Luther's Works, American Edition (56 vols.; St. Louis: Concordia Publishing House and Philadelphia: Fortress Press, 1955–86).

This publication may be available in braille, in large print, or on cassette tape for the visually impaired. Please allow 8 to 12 weeks for delivery. Write to Lutheran Blind Mission, 7550 Watson Rd., St. Louis, MO 63119-4409; call toll-free 1-888-215-2455; or visit the Web site: www.blindmission.org.

Manufactured in the United States of America

1 2 3 4 5 6 7 8 9 10   16 15 14 13 12 11 10 09 08 07

Contents

About This Series 4
Student Introduction 5
An Overview of Christian Denominations 6
Lutheran Facts 9
    Baptism and Priesthood 10
    The Priesthood at Worship 14
    The Priesthood at Work 18
    The Office of the Holy Ministry 22
    Qualities and Tasks 26
    Call and Ordination 30
Leader Guide Introduction 34
    Answers 35
Appendix of Lutheran Teaching 60
Glossary 64

Hymnal Key
LSB=Lutheran Service Book
ELH=Evangelical Lutheran Hymnary
CW=Christian Worship
LW=Lutheran Worship
LBW=Lutheran Book of Worship
TLH=The Lutheran Hymnal

About This Series

"So, what's the deal?"

"What do you mean?"

"Well, you Lutherans say that every Christian is a priest to God, but you have ministers dressed up in fancy robes who speak on behalf of God."

"That's true. Our pastors speak in the stead and by the command of Jesus Christ."

"But doesn't every Christian do that? I just don't get it."

As Lutherans interact with other Christians, they often find themselves struggling to explain their beliefs and practices. Although many Lutherans have learned the "what" of the doctrines of the Church, they do not always have a full scriptural foundation to share the "why." When confronted with different doctrines, they cannot clearly state their faith, much less understand the differences.

Because of insecurities about explaining particular doctrines or practices, some Lutherans may avoid opportunities to share what they have learned from Christ and His Word. The Lutheran Difference Bible study series will identify how Lutherans differ from other Christians and show from the Bible why Lutherans differ. These studies will prepare Lutherans to share their faith and help non-Lutherans understand the Lutheran difference.

Student Introduction

Priesthood and ministry—it seems so simple in theory. Every Christian is a member of Christ's holy priesthood by virtue of his or her Baptism. Some members of the holy priesthood are called and ordained to be pastors in the Office of the Holy Ministry. As our Lutheran Confessions so clearly state: "Our churches teach that no one should publicly teach in the Church, or administer the Sacraments, without a rightly ordered call." (*Augsburg Confession* XIV 1). That appears to be simple enough to understand. While every baptized believer is a priest in the royal priesthood of Jesus Christ, not every Christian holds the Office of the Holy Ministry. Martin Luther put it very succinctly, when he wrote to the Senate of Prague in 1523: "A priest is not the same as a presbyter or minister; one is born, the other is made."

The proper distinction of priesthood and ministry lies at the heart of the Lutheran Reformation. In Luther's day, priests (i.e., ministers or pastors) were seen as a more holy group of Christians, closer to God and separated from the people. They had special power by virtue of their ordination, to change the bread and wine into the body and blood of Christ in the Lord's Supper. They also offered the body and blood of Christ to the Father as an unbloody sacrifice to atone for the sins of the people. Priests were seen as analogous to the Old Testament priesthood of the tabernacle and the temple, a holy order set apart to make sacrifices for the people.

Luther and the reformers realized that the New Testament does not have a priesthood like that of the Old Testament. Jesus Christ is the one and only High Priest of a new covenant, established by the sacrifice that He made on the cross. This once-for-all sacrifice of Christ as the Lamb of God who takes away the sin of the world put an end to all bloody sacrifices for sin. And it ended the Old Testament priesthood of the sons of Aaron. Christ, our High Priest, has an eternal priesthood like that of Melchizedek. And now, every Christian is anointed a priest in Baptism, not to offer bloody sacrifices for sin but to offer his or her body as a living sacrifice in thanksgiving to God.

Luther and the reformers also recognized that the Church as a priesthood has an ordered ministry, an office that is charged with publicly preaching the Word and administering the gifts of Christ's sacrifice. Priesthood and ministry—both are gifts of God to His holy people and through His people to the world.

An Overview of Christian Denominations

The following outline of Christian history will help you understand where the different denominations come from and how they are related to one another. Use this outline in connection with the "Comparisons" sections found throughout the study. Statements of belief for the different churches were drawn from their official confessional writings.

The Great Schism

Eastern Orthodox: On July 16, 1054, Cardinal Humbert entered the Cathedral of the Holy Wisdom in Constantinople just before the worship service. He stepped to the altar and left a letter condemning Michael Cerularius, patriarch of Constantinople. Cerularius responded by condemning the letter and its authors. In that moment, Christian churches of the East and West were severed from one another. Their disagreements centered on what bread could be used in the Lord's Supper and the addition of the *filioque* statement to the Nicene Creed.

The Reformation

Lutheran: On June 15, 1520, Pope Leo X wrote a letter condemning Dr. Martin Luther for his 95 Theses. Luther's theses had challenged the sale of indulgences, a fund-raising effort to pay for the building of St. Peter's Cathedral in Rome. The letter charged Luther with heresy and threatened to excommunicate him if he did not retract his writings within sixty days. Luther replied by publicly burning the letter. Leo excommunicated him on January 3 and condemned all who agreed with Luther or supported his cause.

Reformed: In 1522, the preaching of Ulrich Zwingli in Zurich, Switzerland, convinced people to break their traditional Lenten fast. Also, Zwingli preached that priests should be allowed to marry. When local friars challenged these departures from Medieval Church practice, the Zurich Council supported Zwingli and agreed that the Bible should guide Christian doctrine and practice. Churches of this Reformed tradition include Presbyterians and Episcopalians.

Anabaptist: In January 1525, Conrad Grebel, a follower of Ulrich Zwingli, rebaptized Georg Blaurock. Blaurock began rebaptizing others and founded the Swiss Brethren. Their insistence on adult believers' Baptisms distinguished them from other churches of the Reformation. Anabaptists attracted social extremists who advocated violence in the cause of Christ, complete pacifism, or communal living. Mennonites, Brethren, and Amish churches descend from this movement.

The Counter Reformation

Roman Catholic: When people call the Medieval Church "Roman Catholic," they make a common historical mistake. Roman Catholicism emerged after the Reformation. As early as 1518, Luther and other reformers had appealed to the pope and requested a council to settle the issue of indulgences. Their requests were hindered or denied for a variety of theological and political reasons. Finally, on December 13, 1545, thirty-four leaders from the churches who opposed the Reformation gathered at the invitation of Pope Paul III. They began the Council of Trent (1545–1563), which established the doctrine and practice of Roman Catholicism.

Post-Reformation Movements

Baptist: In 1608 or 1609, John Smyth, a former pastor of the Church of England, baptized himself by pouring water over his head. He formed a congregation of English Separatists in Holland who opposed the rule of bishops and infant Baptism. This marked the start of the English Baptist churches, which remain divided doctrinally over the theology of John Calvin (Particular Baptists) and Jacob Arminius (General Baptists). In the 1800s, the Restoration Movement of Alexander Campbell, a former Presbyterian minister, adopted many Baptist teachings. These churches include the Disciples of Christ (Christian Churches) and the Churches of Christ.

Wesleyan: In 1729, John and Charles Wesley gathered with three other men to study the Scripture, receive Communion, and discipline one another according to the so-called method laid down in the Bible. Later, John Wesley's preaching caused religious revivals in England and America. Methodists, Wesleyans, Nazarenes, and Pentecostals form the Wesleyan family of churches.

Liberal: In 1799, Friedrich Schleiermacher published *Addresses on Religion* in an attempt to make Christianity appealing to people influenced by Rationalism. He argued that religion is not a body of doctrines, provable truths, or a system of ethics but belongs to the realm of feelings. His ideas did not form a new denomination but deeply influenced Christian thinking. Denominations most thoroughly affected by liberalism are the United Church of Christ, Disciples of Christ, and Unitarianism.

Lutheran Facts

All who worship the Holy Trinity and trust in Jesus Christ for the forgiveness of sins are regarded by Lutherans as fellow Christians despite denominational differences.

Lutheran churches first described themselves as *evangelische* or evangelical churches. Opponents of these churches called them *Lutheran* after Dr. Martin Luther, the sixteenth-century German Church reformer.

Lutherans are not disciples of Dr. Martin Luther but disciples of Jesus Christ. They proudly accept the name *Lutheran* because they agree with Dr. Luther's teaching from the Bible as summarized in Luther's Small Catechism.

Nearly every Christian group has some form of the Office of the Holy Ministry. Even the most independent congregations have pastors, some of whom hold considerable authority.

Still there are considerable differences and questions among Christians regarding the priesthood of Christians and the Office of the Holy Ministry. Is every Christian a minister in the same sense that every Christian is a priest? What are the distinctive duties and authorities of the Holy Ministry? How is the concept of priesthood different from ministry? How does God call a person to the Holy Ministry, and who is eligible to serve?

As with many other issues at the time of the Reformation, Luther and his fellow reformers steered a careful path between the Roman Church on the one hand and the radical reformers on the other. Affirming both priesthood and ministry, the Lutheran Reformation retained both the dignity of every Christian before God as a priest and the special office in the Church that is charged with preaching the Word and administering the Sacraments. Unlike Rome, the Lutherans held that every Christian is a member of the priestly caste. Unlike the radical Anabaptists and others, Lutherans held that not everyone is called to be a minister or pastor in the church. In this way, Lutherans preserved both scriptural teachings without compromising one for the sake of the other.

To prepare for the first session of this study, "Baptism and Priesthood," please read 1 Peter 2:1–12.

Baptism and Priesthood

"For a priest, especially in the New Testament, was not made but born. He was created, not ordained. He was born not indeed of flesh, but through a birth of the Spirit, by water and Spirit in the washing of regeneration."

—Martin Luther, "Concerning the Ministry" (AE 40:19)

When you think of a priest, what images come to your mind? A holy man, perhaps, set apart from the rest? Someone who wears long robes and black shirts with a white-tabbed collar? A religious person who is close to God? But do you think of a little child, or a mother caring for her baby, or a car mechanic servicing a transmission, or a farmer tending his crops? Those activities somehow don't seem very priestly, do they? Yet, they are! One of the great insights of the Reformation was that every baptized believer in Jesus Christ is a priest to God in the priesthood of Christ.

1. How do the words *priest* and *priesthood* apply to your own life? Do they affect how you see your daily work? How might you see your life and work differently as you see yourself as a priest to God in Christ's priesthood?

Baptismal Beginnings

2. Read 1 Peter 1:1–2:3; 3:13–22. What evidence can you find that the apostle Peter is writing this letter to newly baptized Christians?

3. Read 1 Peter 2:4–5. What does Peter say about his readers' relationship to God? What Old Testament images does Peter use for these

newly baptized Christians? What is the purpose of being a holy priesthood?

4. Read 1 Peter 2:9–10; Revelation 1:4–6. What are baptized believers called in these passages? What is the importance of each term, and how is it connected to Christ and to Holy Baptism?

5. Read Exodus 19:3–6, and compare it with 1 Peter 2:9–10. How is the Church similar to Old Testament Israel? How was Old Testament Israel baptized?

6. Read Hosea 1:6, 9; 2:1, 22–23, and compare with 1 Peter 2:10. In what ways were we once not God's people and not recipients of mercy? How can you be certain that you are part of the people of God and recipients of His mercy?

7. Read the following passages: Romans 6:1–7; Ephesians 5:26; Galatians 3:27; Titus 3:5; 1 Peter 3:21. What does Baptism accomplish according to these passages? What does this mean for our priesthood in Christ?

Holy Priests in a Priesthood

In the Old Testament, priests were considered holy, that is, set apart by God for service to Him and to His people. The high priest wore special clothing showing that he represented Israel before God and God before Israel (Exodus 28). He had a headpiece with the phrase "Holy to the LORD written on it (Exodus 28:36), a visible reminder of his being set apart for priestly service. The high priest and his priesthood were specially consecrated for their office by washing, anointing with oil, and sacrifice (Exodus 29).

8. Read Exodus 28. What did the high priest wear, and what was the significance of each item of clothing? See Galatians 3:27. How are New Testament priests clothed?

9. Read Exodus 29. How were priests consecrated? How is Baptism an anointing into the priesthood of Christ?

A Greater Priest

The Book of Hebrews makes the argument that Jesus is a superior priest in a greater priesthood than that of the Old Testament.

10. Read Hebrews 4:14–15; 7:11–28; 8:3–6; 9:11–28. How is Jesus a greater High Priest than the high priest of the Old Testament?

11. In light of the differences you found in number 10, what difference might you expect to find in God's New Testament priesthood compared with the Old Testament?

Comparisons

Eastern Orthodox: "What ecclesiastical institution is there through which the succession of the Apostolical ministry is preserved? The ecclesiastical *Hierarchy*" (*The Longer Catechism of the Eastern Church,* Question 276).

Lutheran: "Here belong the statements of Christ that testify that the Keys have been given to the Church, and not merely to certain persons, 'Where two or three are gathered in My name . . .' [Matthew 18:20]. Finally, Peter's statement also confirms this, 'You are . . . a royal priesthood' [1 Peter 2:9]" (*The Power and the Primacy of the Pope* 68–69).

Reformed/Presbyterian: "All saints that are united to Jesus Christ their head, by his Spirit and by faith, have fellowship with him in his graces, sufferings, death, resurrection, and glory: and being united to one another in love, they have communion in each other's gifts and graces, and are obliged to the performance of such duties, public and private, as do conduce to their mutual good, both in the inward and outward man" (*The Westminster Confession of Faith* XXVI 1).

Roman Catholic: "If any one saith, that there is not in the New Testament a visible and external priesthood; or, that there is not any power of consecrating and offering the true body and blood of the Lord, and of forgiving and retaining sins, but only an office and bare ministry of preaching the Gospel; or, that those who do not preach are not priests at all: let him be anathema" (*The Canons and Decrees of the Council of Trent* IV 1).

Baptist: "The members of these churches are saints by calling, visibly manifesting and evidencing (in and by their profession and walking) their obedience unto that call of Christ" (*The Baptist Confession of 1688*, 6).

Point to Remember

But you are a royal priesthood, a holy nation, a people for His own possession, that you may proclaim the excellencies of Him who called you out of darkness into His marvelous light. 1 Peter 2:9

To prepare for the next section, "The Priesthood at Worship," read Romans 12:1–21.

The Priesthood at Worship

Life is worship. The real issue in worship is set between idolatry, which is death, and faith, which is participation in the life of God.

—Kenneth F. Korby, "The Church at Worship" in *The Lively Function of the Gospel*

Priests worship, and a priesthood is a worshiping community. Strictly speaking, worship is a two-way street. The Lord serves His people through His Word, and His people serve Him through their prayers and praise. These two ways we commonly call Sacrament and sacrifice. Sacraments run from God to us; sacrifices run from us to God. In the Old Testament, these were sacrifices of blood, grain, wine, or money. In the New Testament, the sacrifices are unbloody, offered not for sin, but in thanksgiving for what God has done. Like smoke rising up from the altar, the sacrifices of God's priestly people rise up to Him.

12. Think of all that goes on in the worship of God. What are some of the sacrificial activities we offer to God?

Spiritual Sacrifices

13. Read Romans 12:1–2. What offering do the priests of the New Testament make? What makes the spiritual sacrifices of God's priesthood acceptable to Him?

14. Read Romans 12:3–8. What is the relationship of the individual priest to the entire priesthood? Does everyone have the same gifts and responsibilities? Why is diversity of gifts and responsibilities a good thing for the priesthood (see 1 Corinthians 12:12–30)?

15. Read Colossians 3:12–17. How does Paul describe the baptismal clothing of God's chosen people? What virtues does Paul commend? To what activities does Paul call the congregation of priests?

16. Read Colossians 3:16. How does the Word of Christ dwell richly among God's people? How do these things happen in your congregation? in your home?

17. Read 1 Peter 2:9. What activities might be included in the phrase "that you may proclaim the excellencies of Him who called you out of darkness into His marvelous light"?

18. Read Hebrews 12:18–29. In this passage, the author compares Mount Sinai of the old covenant to Mount Zion of the new. List seven things we come to when we gather for worship. What then should the attitude of the worshiping priesthood be in view of these gifts?

"Worthy Is the Lamb"

Revelation 4 and 5 give a marvelous depiction of worship from a heavenly perspective. They give a foretaste of what is to come and a revelation of the mystery of worship that already is.

19. Read Revelation 4 and 5. Who is at the very center of worship? How does He appear? Who are the worshipers in this heavenly congregation (see Revelation 4:4, 6; 5:11)? Whom do they represent, and what is the basis of their praise?

20. In light of the heavenly worship depicted in Revelation, discuss this statement: "Christian worship always has Jesus Christ at the center."

Everything in Order

Worship is an ordered event. That shouldn't be surprising. Most human activities are. When we go to a ball game, we sit in assigned seats, and the players play their assigned positions. The ordered activity of worship is no different.

21. Read 1 Corinthians 14:26–39. Apparently, the Corinthian congregation had some problems with disorderly conduct in worship. What problems do you detect? What rules does Paul lay down?

22. How does the liturgy, that is, an ordered pattern of worship, provide that everything is done in a fitting and orderly way?

23. As a priest in Christ's royal priesthood, what is your place and purpose in worship?

Comparisons

Eastern Orthodox: "Whence originates the Hierarchy of the Orthodox Christian Church? From Jesus Christ himself, and from the descent of the Holy Ghost on the Apostles; from which time it is continued, in unbroken succession, through the laying on of hands, in the Sacrament of Orders" (*The Longer Catechism of the Eastern Church*, Question 277).

Lutheran: "So that we may obtain this faith, the ministry of teaching the Gospel and administering the Sacraments was instituted.

Through the Word and Sacraments, as through instruments, the Holy Spirit is given [John 20:22]" (*Augsburg Confession* V). "Our churches teach that no one should publicly teach in the Church, or administer the Sacraments, without a rightly ordered call" (*Augsburg Confession* XIV).

Reformed/Presbyterian: "Saints, by profession, are bound to maintain an holy fellowship and communion in the worship of God, and in performing such other spiritual services as tend to their mutual edification; as also in relieving each other in outward things, according to their several abilities and necessities" (*The Westminster Confession of Faith* XXVI 2).

Roman Catholic: "If anyone saith, that order, or sacred ordination, is not truly and properly a sacrament instituted by Christ the Lord; or, that it is a kind of human figment devised by men unskilled in ecclesiastical matters; or, that it is only a kind of rite for choosing ministers of the Word of God and of the sacraments: let him be anathema" (*The Canons and Decrees of the Council of Trent* IV 3).

Baptist: "To each of these churches thus gathered, according to his mind declared in his Word, he hath given all that power and authority which is any way needful for the carrying on that order in worship and discipline which he hath instituted for them to observe, with commands and rules for the due and right exerting and executing of that power" (*The Baptist Confession of 1688*, 7).

Point to Remember

I appeal to you therefore, brothers, by the mercies of God, to present your bodies as a living sacrifice, holy and acceptable to God, which is your spiritual worship. Romans 12:1

To prepare for the next session, "The Priesthood at Work," read Ephesians 5:1–20.

The Priesthood at Work

We conclude therefore that a Christian man does not live in himself, but in Christ and in his neighbor, or else is no Christian: in Christ by faith; in his neighbor by love.

—Martin Luther, *The Freedom of the Christian* (AE 31:371)

One of the great contributions of the Lutheran Reformation is the concept, derived from God's Word, of vocation or calling. Every Christian has a calling from God, defined by where God has located you in relation to those He has placed around you. There each Christian as a priest to God serves his or her neighbor, and in so doing, serves God Himself.

This means that priestly work goes on not only in church but also in the home, the workplace, and the community in which the priest lives. A helpful guide for the work of the priesthood in vocation is the "Table of Christian Responsibilities" in the Small Catechism. There, the life of the priest is organized in three areas: church; civil society; and home, and by extension, the workplace.

24. Before we begin this section, it will be helpful to get our bearings. Where has God located you with respect to home, congregation, and community? Whom has God placed around you as your neighbor in terms of family, friends, congregation, and neighborhood? What are the various hats that you currently wear?

Priests in Church, Home, and Community

25. Read 1 Corinthians 9:14; Galatians 6:6–7; 1 Timothy 5:17–18; 1 Thessalonians 5:12–13; Hebrews 13:17. What do the priests of God owe their pastors? What part do you play in each of these?

26. Read Ephesians 5:22–6:4; 1 Peter 3:1–7. As priests to God, how are husbands to serve their wives? How are wives to serve their hus-

bands? How are children to serve their parents and parents to serve their children?

27. Read Ephesians 6:5–9. What is the priesthood of the Christian worker toward his or her boss? What is the priesthood of the Christian boss toward his or her worker? How does this affect their work?

28. Read Romans 13:1–7; Titus 3:1; 1 Peter 2:13–14. What is the Christian's priestly service toward the government? What do Christians owe the governing authority?

29. Read 1 Timothy 2:1–3. Intercession for others is a uniquely priestly work. Why is it important that Christians pray for those in government regardless of political party?

30. Read Acts 5:27–32. Is it ever proper for a Christian to disobey the government? How does one go about deciding?

To Whom It Is Given

31. Read 1 Samuel 13:1–13. How was Saul unfaithful to his calling as king? Does the end ever justify the means, even when it seems expedient?

32. Read Hebrews 5:4–6. Who called Jesus to be the High Priest of the world? If Jesus did not take this honor upon Himself, what does this have to say about our priesthood and our vocation?

Priestly Perfection

33. Consider this quote from the Augsburg Confession: "True Christian perfection is to fear God from the heart, to have great faith, and to trust that for Christ's sake we have a God who has been reconciled [2 Corinthians 5:18–19]. It means to ask for and expect from God His help in all things with confident assurance that we are to live according to our calling in life, being diligent in outward good works, serving in our calling" (*Augsburg Confession* XXVII 49). How does the idea of priesthood influence the way you see your calling?

Comparisons

Eastern Orthodox: "What are *Orders*? Orders are a Sacrament, in which the Holy Ghost, by the laying on of the Bishop's hands, ordains them that be rightly chosen to minister sacraments, and to feed the flock of Christ" (*The Longer Catechism of the Eastern Church*, Question 357).

Lutheran: "Therefore, when the regular bishops become enemies of the Church or are unwilling to administer ordination, the churches retain their own right [to ordain their own ministers]. Wherever the Church is, there is the authority to administer the Gospel" (*The Power and the Primacy of the Pope* 66–67).

Reformed/Presbyterian: "The Lord Jesus, as king and head of his Church, hath therein appointed a government in the hand of Church officers, distinct from the civil magistrate" (*The Westminster Confession of Faith* XXX 1).

Roman Catholic: "If anyone saith, that, by sacred ordination, the Holy Ghost is not given; and that vainly therefore do the bishops say, *Receive ye the Holy Ghost;* or, that a character is not imprinted by that ordination; or, that he who has once been a priest can again become a layman: let him be anathema" *The Canons and Decrees of the Council of Trent* IV 4).

Baptist: "A particular church gathered and completely organized, according to the mind of Christ, consists of officers and members; and the officers appointed by Christ to be chosen and set apart by the Church (so-called and gathered) for the peculiar administration of ordinances, and execution of power and duty, which he intrusts them with or calls them to, to be continued to the end of the world, are bishops or elders and deacons" (*The Baptist Confession of 1688*, 8).

Point to Remember

[Submit] to one another out of reverence for Christ. Ephesians 5:21

To prepare for the next session, "The Office of the Holy Ministry," read Ephesians 4:1–13.

The Office of the Holy Ministry

The ministry of the Word, or the preaching office, is not a human institution but an office that God Himself has established.

—C. F. W. Walther, "Thesis II on the Office" from *Church and Ministry*

When we hear the word *authority*, we usually we think of the law, judges in black robes, and police officers with guns. In the Bible, the word *authority* is actually derived from the word *permission*. Authority, as it is used in the Scriptures, is permission granted to someone to do something. This is where we get the notion of the office. Authority doesn't float in the air like gas but is located in an office, enabling a person to do a given task.

We are under the authority of government in civil society and under the authority of parents in the home. Without parents and government, ordered society quickly degenerates into anarchy. Likewise, the Church without the Office of the Holy Ministry is no longer an ordered priesthood but a random collection of individual priests.

34. What are some of the authority structures under which you live? What would happen if there were no notion of office, where literally anyone could be mayor of the city or president of the nation any time he or she felt like it? How is being under authority liberating for your life and work?

Disciples and Apostles

35. Read Mark 3:13–18. Notice that Mark makes a distinction that these twelve disciples were apostles. The word *disciple* means "one who follows or learns from another," while the word *apostle* means "one who is sent with authority." With what authority did Jesus send the Twelve?

36. Read Matthew 28:16–20. On whose authority were the Eleven sent? What activity were they authorized to do? By what means were they given to accomplish this activity? Could the Eleven reasonably be expected to complete their mandate from Jesus?

37. Read Luke 10:16; John 20:23. What promise does Jesus make concerning those He sends with authority? Who is actually speaking when the apostle speaks? Why is this of special comfort to those who hear?

38. Read Romans 10:14–15. What does sending have to do with believing? Why is it important that preachers objectively be sent?

39. Read Acts 1:12–26. Verses 20 and 25 refer to Judas's position as an office that had been vacated and needed to be filled. How is it comforting to know that even though Judas was unfaithful, his apostolic office remained intact? What does this tell us about faithless or wicked pastors and their pastoral acts?

40. Read Ephesians 4:7–13. Does God give all Christians to the Church as pastors? Who gives these gifts? For what purpose and to what end are these gifts given?

41. Read 1 Corinthians 3:5–9. It appears from this passage that Paul preached the Word and Apollos baptized. What does this passage tell you about the interchangeability of pastors? What does Paul call the Corinthian congregation in this passage? Who is actually at work in, with, and under the Holy Ministry?

A Stewardship

A steward is a household office in which someone is responsible to see to it that every servant gets his or her fair share of the household goods (Luke 12:42). The pastoral office is an office of stewardship charged with caring for the household of God and distributing the gifts of Christ to His priesthood.

42. Read 1 Corinthians 4:1–5. A mystery is a hidden thing that must be revealed by the Word of God. As "stewards of God's mysteries," what hidden things does the pastoral office reveal by the Word of God (see 1 Corinthians 15:51; Ephesians 1:9–10; Colossians 2:2; 1 Timothy 3:16)?

43. Read Matthew 26:17–30; 28:16–20; John 20:21–23. To whom did Jesus entrust the gifts of His body and blood, His Baptism, and His forgiveness? What implications does this have for the Office of the Holy Ministry?

Accountability

With authority comes accountability to the one granting the authority. Those who govern are accountable to the people. Parents are held accountable by God for their care of their children. Likewise, pastors are accountable for their stewardship of the Word of God.

44. Read 1 Corinthians 3:10–15. What image does Paul use here for the work of the Holy Ministry? How will the work of a pastor be tested? Is the pastor saved by his work? What if his work is found wanting in some way? What does this mean for pastors and their congregations?

45. Read Acts 20:28–29. The Greek word for *overseer* is the word *episkopos*, commonly translated "bishop." Who makes the pastor an overseer over the flock of God? To whom is the pastor ultimately accountable? Whose Church is it, and what is it worth to God?

46. Read Hebrews 13:17; James 3:1. Why is it important that we give our pastors support and obedience? Is there a situation where we must disobey our pastors? If so, what is the best way to handle this?

Comparisons

Eastern Orthodox: "What is it to feed the Church? To instruct the people in faith, piety, and good works" (*The Longer Catechism of the Eastern Church*, Question 358).

Lutheran: "[The Holy Spirit] works faith, when and where it pleases God [John 3:8], in those who hear the good news that God justifies those who believe that they are received into grace for Christ's sake. This happens not through our own merits, but for Christ's sake" (*Augsburg Confession* V 3).

Reformed/Presbyterian: "To these [Church] officers the keys of the kingdom of heaven are committed, by virtue whereof they have power respectively to retain and remit sins, to shut that kingdom against the impenitent, both by the Word and censures; and to open it unto penitent sinners, by the ministry of the gospel, and by absolution from censures, as occasion shall require" (*The Westminster Confession of Faith* XXX 2).

Roman Catholic: If anyone saith, that, in the Catholic Church there is not a hierarchy by divine ordination instituted, consisting of bishops, priests, and ministers: let him be anathema." (*The Canons and Decrees of the Council of Trent* IV 6).

Baptist: "The way appointed by Christ for the calling of any person, fitted and gifted by the Holy Spirit, unto the office of bishop or elder in the church is that he be chosen thereunto by the common suffrage of the church itself, and solemnly set apart by fasting and prayer, with imposition of hands of the eldership of the church, if there be any before constituted therein; and of a deacon, that he be chosen by the like suffrage, and set apart by prayer, and the like imposition of hands" (*The Baptist Confession of 1688*, 9).

Point to Remember

The one who hears you hears Me, and the one who rejects you rejects Me, and the one who rejects Me rejects Him who sent Me. Luke 10:16

To prepare for the next session, "Qualities and Tasks," read 1 Timothy 3:1–13.

Qualities and Tasks

Show me the man who keeps his house in hand;
he's fit for public authority.
—Sophocles, *Antigone*

An office is never simply bare authority; there are always responsibilities and accountability. There are standards for virtually every office and task in our lives. Not everyone is qualified to be president of the United States. Nor is everyone capable of being a firefighter or a police officer. Some offices require specific gifts, others specific training and experience. Certain situations, such as a criminal conviction, may even disqualify a person from holding a particular office.

The Office of the Holy Ministry also requires certain qualities and abilities of those who are chosen for it, and it lays on them certain duties and responsibilities along with accountability for the execution of that office. The Holy Ministry is not a special kind of priesthood but a particular calling within the royal priesthood of Christians.

47. What are some of the qualities you think are important in a pastor? What do you think are the essential tasks of the Office of the Holy Ministry?

A Noble Task

48. Read 1 Timothy 3:1–13; Titus 1:6–9. (Note: In this passage, the word *deacon* refers to an assistant to the overseer. See also Philippians 1:1.) What are the qualities of the person who desires the office of overseer/elder (pastor), or deacon in the Church? Why is it essential that those who hold these offices have a good reputation both inside and outside the Church?

49. Read 1 Timothy 2:11–15. What reason is cited here for excluding women from the pastoral office (see also 1 Corinthians 14:33–35)?

50. Read 1 Timothy 4:11–14; 2 Timothy 3:14–17. What place do the Scriptures have in the work of the pastoral office? For what are the Scriptures useful for the man of God?

51. Read 2 Timothy 2:15; 4:1–2. What ought to characterize the preaching of the pastoral office?

52. Read 1 Timothy 5:17–20. Note: The term *elder* is synonymous with *overseer* or *pastor* (see Acts 20:17ff). What activities of the pastoral office does Paul cite here? Why might those who govern be worthy of double pay? How are pastors who sin to be dealt with according to this passage?

53. Read 1 Timothy 6:3–10. Why is false doctrine so dangerous in the Church? How do greed and the temptation to become rich undermine the work of the ministry?

The Lord Is My Pastor

In our American Lutheran tradition, the most common title for those who hold the Office of the Holy Ministry is the word *pastor*. This word comes from the Latin *pastores,* which means "shepherd." In Acts 20:28, to be an overseer is to be a shepherd.

54. Read Psalm 23. How might this Good Shepherd psalm inform us about the work of a good pastor? Consider each verse of this psalm as a job description of the good pastor.

55. Read 1 Peter 5:1–4. How are pastors to shepherd their congregations according to this passage? Who is the chief Shepherd under which pastors serve? What promise does He bring?

Preaching and Prayer

The authority of the pastoral office is not a blanket authority to do anything and everything in the Church but to oversee the life of the congregation, to preach, teach, administer the Sacraments, warn, rebuke, and restore. Other tasks can often intrude, diluting the effectiveness of the office.

56. Read Acts 6:1–7. What was the situation in the Jerusalem congregation that caused difficulties for the apostles? What was the solution? What was the focus of the apostles (see v. 4)?

57. In what ways can the Christian congregation free its pastor(s) to do the proper work of the Office of the Holy Ministry? What potential distractions do you see arising in the Church today that could deflect pastors from their focus on the Word of God and prayer?

Comparisons

Eastern Orthodox: "How many necessary *degrees* are there of Orders? Three: those of *Bishop, Priest,* and *Deacon*" (*The Longer Catechism of the Eastern Church*, Question 359).

Lutheran: "Since the grades of bishop and pastor are not different by divine authority, it is clear that ordination administered by a pastor in his own church is valid by divine law" (*The Power and the Primacy of the Pope* 65).

Reformed/Presbyterian: "Church censures are necessary for the reclaiming and gaining of offending brethren; for deterring of others from the like offenses; for purging out of that leaven which might infect the whole lump; for vindicating the honor of Christ, and the holy profession of the gospel; and for preventing the wrath of God, which might justly fall upon the Church, if they should suffer his covenant, and the seals thereof, to be profaned by notorious and obstinate offenders" (*The Westminster Confession of Faith* XXX 3).

Roman Catholic: "If any one saith, that bishops are not superior to priests; or, that they have not the power of confirming and ordaining; or, that the power which they possess is common to them and to priests; or, that orders, conferred by them, without the consent or vocation of the people, or of the secular power, are invalid; or, that those who have neither been rightly ordained, nor sent, by ecclesiastical and canonical power, but come from elsewhere, are lawful ministers of the Word and of the sacraments: let him be anathema" (*The Canon and Decrees of the Council of Trent* IV 7).

Baptist: "The work of pastors being constantly to attend the service of Christ in his churches, in the ministry of the Word and prayer, with watching for their souls, as they that must give an account to him" (*The Baptist Confession of 1688*, 10).

Point to Remember

Do your best to present yourself to God as one approved, a worker who has no need to be ashamed, rightly handling the word of truth. 2 Timothy 2:15

To prepare for the next session, "Call and Ordination," read 1 Timothy 1:3–7.

Call and Ordination

Our churches teach that no one should publicly teach in the Church, or administer the Sacraments, without a rightly ordered call.

—*Augsburg Confession* (XIV)

How do you come into an office? Never on your own! You cannot place yourself into an office; it must be given to you. In America, we choose our public officials by election or by appointment depending on the office, and then they are formally and publicly placed into office by those authorized to do so. For example, the president of the United States is elected on the first Tuesday of November and placed into office with a solemn oath administered by the chief justice on January 20 the next year. Only then is that person rightfully in the office.

The Church, likewise, deals with the Office of the Holy Ministry as a public office. Men are chosen by election or appointment and then are solemnly placed into office with a vow, prayer, and the Word of God. These traditional procedures, handed down from the Early Church, reflect the divine character of the Office of the Holy Ministry. It is the Lord's office, and it is His Church. He calls and ordains certain priests to be pastors in His Church.

58. Think of the various public offices with which you are familiar, whether in political life or even in clubs or other organizations. How are people chosen for office? How are they placed into office? How are people sure that they legitimately hold the offices they claim?

Chosen to Serve

59. Read Acts 1:12–26. What criteria were used to pick candidates to fill the vacancy in the office left by Judas? How was Matthias ultimately selected? Do you think this procedure might be useful in the Church today?

60. Read Acts 6:1–7. Who chose the seven deacons who were appointed to care for the Greek widows? What part did the apostles have in placing them into their office (v. 6)?

61. Read Acts 14:23; Titus 1:5; 2 Timothy 2:2. Who appointed the elders (pastors) in these early congregations?

62. The Lutheran Confessions state that the right to have a pastor may never be denied a congregation, and because the Church alone possesses the priesthood, it has the right to elect and ordain ministers (*The Power and the Primacy of the Pope* 67–69). Historically, this right to elect and ordain has been exercised in various ways. Sometimes, pastors are appointed by bishops or consistories (committees that oversee regions); other times they are elected directly by congregations. What are the pros or cons of the various ways a congregation might choose its pastor?

63. Read Acts 20:28. Who ultimately appoints the pastors in congregations? Why is it important for us to recognize that God is the one who calls through whatever instruments are used?

64. What are some ways congregations might guard against the notion that they are hiring a pastor instead of God calling a pastor through them?

With the Laying on of Hands

The liturgical gesture of laying on of hands is an ancient practice going back to the Old Testament. Moses laid his hands on Joshua to ordain him as his successor (Deuteronomy 34:9). Jesus laid hands on people for healing and for blessing. The laying on of hands is a sign of specificity, indicating that a particular person is being prayed for or blessed.

65. Read Acts 6:5–6. Who laid hands on the men chosen as deacons, and what purpose did it serve?

66. Read 1 Timothy 4:14; 2 Timothy 1:6–7. Who laid hands on Timothy, and what was accomplished by the laying on of hands? What were the gifts received through the laying on of hands?

Ordained

Ordination is a liturgical rite by which a person who has been previously called is publicly placed into office. It is the churchly equivalent of inauguration in the political realm.

67. Read 2 Timothy 1:6–7. How would Timothy's ordination bring comfort and confidence to this young pastor in the midst of great trial and testing? Read 1 Timothy 5:22. Why would it be unwise to be hasty in ordaining men to the pastoral office?

68. Ordination is traditionally done by neighboring pastors outside the congregation. How does this practice underscore the fact that a pastor is a gift of the ascended Christ to His congregation (see Ephesians 4:11)?

Comparisons

Eastern Orthodox: "What difference is there between them [bishop, priest, and deacon]? The Deacon serves at the Sacraments; the Priest hallows Sacraments in dependence on the Bishop; the bishop not only hallows the Sacraments himself, but has power also to impart to others, by the laying on of his hands, the gift and grace to hallow them" (*The Longer Catechism of the Eastern Church,* Question 360).

Lutheran: "Wherever the Church is, there is the authority to administer the Gospel. Therefore, it is necessary for the Church to retain the authority to call, elect, and ordain ministers. This authority is a gift that in reality is given to the Church. No human power can take this gift away from the Church" (*The Power and Primacy of the Pope* 67).

Reformed/Presbyterian: "For the better attaining of these ends, the officers of the Church are to proceed by admonition, suspension from the Sacrament of the Lord's Supper for a season, and by excommunication from the Church, according to the nature of the crime and demerit of the person" (*The Westminster Confession of Faith* XXX 4).

Roman Catholic: "If any one saith, that the bishops, who are assumed by authority of the Roman Pontiff, are not legitimate and true bishops, but are a human figment: let him be anathema" (*The Canons and Decrees of the Council of Trent* IV 8).

Baptist: "Although it be incumbent on the bishops or pastors of the churches to be instant in preaching the Word by way of office, yet the work of preaching the Word is not so peculiarly confined to them by that others also, gifted and fitted by the Holy Spirit for it, and approved and called by the Church, may and ought to perform it" (*The Baptist Confession of 1688*, 11).

Point to Remember

For this reason I remind you to fan into flame the gift of God, which is in you through the laying on of my hands, for God gave us a spirit not of fear but of power and love and self-control. 2 Timothy 1:6

Leader Guide

Leaders, please note the different abilities of your class members. Some will easily find the many passages listed in this study. Others will struggle to find even the "easy" passages. To help everyone participate, team up members of the class. For example, if a question asks you to look up several passages, assign one passage to one group, the second to another, and so on. Divide up the work. Let participants present the different answers they discover.

Each topic is divided into four easy-to-use sections.

Focus: Key concepts that will be discovered.

Inform: Guides the participants into Scripture to uncover truth concerning a doctrine.

Connect: Enables participants to apply that which is learned in Scripture to their lives, and provides them an opportunity to formulate and articulate a defense of a key doctrine.

Vision: Provides participants with practical suggestions for extending the theme of the lesson out of the classroom and into the world.

Baptism and Priesthood

Objectives

By the power of the Holy Spirit working through God's Word, participants will (1) understand that they are anointed priests to God in Holy Baptism, (2) see their lives in Baptism as a priesthood, and (3) see themselves as priests to God under the high priesthood of Jesus Christ.

Opening Worship

Read Psalm 110 together. Then sing "Baptized into Your Name Most Holy" (*LSB* 590; *ELH* 242; *CW* 294; *LW* 224; *LBW* 192; *TLH* 298) or "Church of God, Elect and Glorious" (*LSB* 646).

Prayer: Gracious God, our heavenly Father, grant that as You have anointed us to be kings and priests in the kingdom and priesthood of Your beloved Jesus Christ, our Savior, we may serve in His righteousness and holiness all the days of our lives, through Jesus Christ, our Lord. Amen.

Focus

1. Answers will vary. The purpose of this question is to get people to talk about how they view *priest* and *priesthood*. Important are any expressions that recognize even the most menial of tasks as holy when done by a priest to God.

Baptismal Beginnings (Inform)

2. This is an exercise in reading between the lines. There are many baptismal references in 1 Peter. Among them are 1:3 (new birth); 1:23 (born again); 2:2 (newborn babies); 2:9 (Exodus reference); 3:21 (Baptism saves you).

3. They are "chosen by God" and "precious to Him." Peter speaks of them as a "spiritual house" (i.e., temple) and a "holy priesthood." Both of these are images from the Old Testament, referring to the Levitical priesthood and the tabernacle or temple (see Exodus 37–39). The purpose of the New Testament priesthood is to offer "spiritual sacrifices" that are acceptable to God through Jesus Christ. This stands in contrast to

the sacrifices of the Old Testament, which were sacrifices of blood for the atonement of sin.

4. The baptized are called a chosen people, royal priesthood, holy nation, God's possession, and kings and priests (Revelation 1:4–6). Chosen implies election in grace; royal priesthood suggests kingly, sacrificial service; holy nation says that the Church is the New Testament Israel of God (Galatians 6:16). Each is granted in Christ through Holy Baptism.

5. Israel and the Church both come through water (Red Sea and Baptism) and into the Promised Land as God's holy nation and priesthood. Israel's "baptism" was in the Red Sea under Moses' guidance, since he was the covenant leader (1 Corinthians 10:2).

6. Hosea's two children of Gomer's adultery were called Lo-Ruhamah ("not loved") and Lo-Ammi ("not my people"). Our sin and the sin of Adam have alienated us from God and placed us under His wrath. In Baptism, God restores us in Christ, the beloved Son, so that we are beloved and belong to God as His priestly people.

7. Baptism joins us to Christ in His death, washes us with the Word, clothes us with Christ, works rebirth and renewal by the Holy Spirit, and saves us through the death and resurrection of Jesus. This means we are born again and clothed for a life of priestly service to God, to live under Christ in His Kingdom, and to serve Him, as it says in the Small Catechism, in "everlasting righteousness, innocence, and blessedness." Our priestly vestments are the righteousness of Christ, which we wear as a robe covering our sin.

Holy Priests in a Priesthood (Connect)

8. The high priest wore a breastplate, ephod, robe, tunic, sash, and turban. The breastplate and ephod indicated that he represented the people before God; the turban with its insignia indicated that he represented God before the people. Paul states that in Baptism we are clothed with Christ, that is, we wear the vestments of Jesus Christ, our High Priest, as priests in His royal priesthood.

9. A priest was washed with water and anointed with oil. Sacrifices were made at priests' ordinations, and blood was sprinkled on them. In Baptism, we are cleansed by the blood of Christ and anointed by Him as priests to serve Him. As 1 Peter 2:9 indicates, Baptism is a consecration into the royal priesthood, wherein Christ anoints us for priestly service.

A Greater Priest (Vision)

10. Hebrews makes the argument that Christ is superior to the Old Testament priesthood of Aaron. Christ is a sinless High Priest in a greater

order (Melchizedek, not Aaron), who offers His blood in a greater and superior sacrifice in a greater covenant at a greater, eternal tabernacle.

11. Given that Christ's priesthood is eternal, we would expect the New Testament priesthood to reflect the once-for-all character of Jesus' priestly sacrifice. No longer is the shedding of blood called for in the New Testament, because the atoning blood of Christ has been shed one time for all time. The priesthood of the New Testament does not deal with the atonement for sin but with offerings of thanksgiving in view of Christ's all-atoning sacrifice. The Apology states clearly:

> "These are the sacrifices of the New Testament, as Peter teaches, 'a holy priesthood, to offer spiritual sacrifices' (1 Peter 2:5). Spiritual sacrifices, however, are contrasted not only with those of cattle, but even with human works offered by the outward act, because *spiritual* refers to the movements of the Holy Spirit in us." (*Apology of the Augsburg Confession* XXIV 26)

The Priesthood at Worship

Objectives

By the power of the Holy Spirit working through God's Word, participants will (1) learn that the priesthood of the baptized involves worship, (2) believe that this priestly worship is centered in Jesus Christ who is both priest and sacrifice, and (3) see that this worship is an ordered event in which every priest has his or her own place and purpose.

Opening Worship

Read Psalm 132 together. Then, sing "At the Lamb's High Feast We Sing (*LSB* 633; *ELH* 310; *CW* 141; *LW* 126; *LBW* 210) or "Praise the Almighty" (*LSB* 797; *ELH* 497; *CW* 235; *LW* 445; *LBW* 539; *TLH* 26).

Prayer: Gracious God, our heavenly Father, You have called and gathered us to worship in the name of Your Son, the Lamb who was slain but lives and whose blood has redeemed us from sin and death. Grant that we may worship You without fear and declare the praises of Him who called us out of darkness into His marvelous light, Jesus Christ, our Lord. Amen.

Focus

12. The focus is on worship and the various activities in the liturgy. The various sacrificial actions include prayer, confession, praise, and the singing of hymns. Sacramental actions include hearing the Word and receiving the Sacrament, and so on. The priestly direction of worship goes from us to God, while the sacramental direction of worship runs from God to us. This is in important distinction in a Lutheran understanding of worship (see *Apology of the Augsburg Confession* XXIV 16).

Spiritual Sacrifices (Inform)

13. Priests in the New Testament offer their bodies as living sacrifices, which are their spiritual worship. Notice that spiritual does not mean non-material or having nothing to do with the body. Rather, the word *spiritual* means, as the Confessions state, that which is worked by the Holy Spirit (*Apology of the Augsburg Confession* XXIV 26). The sacrifices are living, since the one sacrifice into death that atones for all

sin has been accomplished in the cross of Jesus. It is this sacrifice, once for all, that makes the spiritual sacrifices of God's priestly people acceptable to Him. They are offered in view of God's mercy in Jesus Christ.

14. An individual priest is to the priesthood as a member is to the whole body. This is a very important concept. No person is a priest unto himself or herself but a priest *within a priesthood.* Just as a body has a diversity of parts with differing functions, so the priesthood of Christ has several priests with a diversity of duties and gifts. In Romans, Paul specifically lists prophesying (in the sense of proclaiming the Word), serving, teaching, encouraging, contributing, leading, and showing mercy. In 1 Corinthians, he lists apostles, prophets, and teachers, followed by workers of miracles, healers, administrators, those speaking in various tongues, and the like. This is clearly not intended as some comprehensive inventory of gifts, but these are examples of how the Spirit arranges a diversity of gifts in a given congregation for the common good. Every baptized believer has a place and purpose in the priesthood of Christ, and no task or gift is insignificant or unimportant. This diversity of gifts and persons strengthens the priesthood by placing a variety of resources at the disposal of the Holy Spirit who unites all believers in the one body of Christ.

15. The priestly vestments of Christ's people are not vestments made of cloth but are the robe of Christ's righteousness and His perfect obedience under the Law. Paul describes these priestly vestments as compassion, kindness, humility, gentleness, and patience. These all describe Christ and the baptized believer in Christ. In addition, Paul commends the virtues of forgiveness and love, which preserve the unity of the priesthood. Without forgiveness and love, the priests of God would not be united as a priesthood. The priesthood as a united whole, forgiving each other and uniting in love, is called to peace, to thanksgiving, to teaching, and to admonishing each other with the Word of Christ through psalms, hymns, and spiritual songs.

16. The Word of Christ dwells richly among God's people as they teach and admonish each other in the wisdom of Christ and sing psalms, hymns, and spiritual songs together. The liturgy guides and shapes this priestly praise in the congregation, and the daily offices of prayer and the Word do the same in the Christian household. Here, the disciplines of daily prayer, as taught in the Small Catechism, are of special importance, as the priests of God pray together as a family, where the father presides and the mother assists in the instruction and prayers of the children.

17. "Declaring the praises of Christ" would include the singing of hymns, witnessing to others, proclaiming the Gospel to one another, and showing the mercy of Christ to those in need in our various callings.

18. Hebrews lists seven things that pertain to the greater worship of the New Testament: (1) Mount Zion, the heavenly Jerusalem, the city of God; (2) countless angels; (3) the assembly of the firstborn; (4) the judge of all; (5) the spirits of the justified; (6) Jesus, the mediator of a new covenant; (7) His sprinkled blood. These are all given as a present tense reality, not something that will happen in the future. This is the present tense reality of Christian worship, which has much more to it than meets the eye. In view of these gifts, Hebrews 12:29 states that we are to worship God with reverence (fear) and awe, "for our God is a consuming fire." Priestly worship is never comfortable, but it is comforting. To enter into the presence of God is an awe-full experience, because He can destroy you, and He can save you.

"Worthy Is the Lamb" (Connect)

19. Revelation gives a glimpse into the worship of heaven. At the center of worship is the Lamb, enthroned in the very center of throne, who appears slain and alive at the same time. Surrounding the Lamb (Christ) are twenty-four enthroned elders, representing the Church as God's Israel, both Old and New Testament. At the four corners are the four living ones, the seraphim that Isaiah saw when he was called (Isaiah 6), now with faces uncovered. Their faces reflect their constituencies—an eagle, the foremost creature of the air; an ox, the chief domestic beast; a lion, the chief of the wild beasts; and a man, the head of the creation. Together, they represent the whole creation that worships the Father and the Son in the Holy Spirit. Around them are myriads of angels who chant an endless hymn to Christ: "Worthy is the Lamb who was slain." The hymns of this heavenly praise rest on two pillars—creation and redemption. God is praised as Creator, "for You created all things, and by Your will they existed and were created" (Revelation 4:11). And He is praised for the work of redemption through His Son: "with your blood you purchased men for God from every tribe and language and people and nation." Creation and redemption are the twin pillars on which all of worship rests. It is centered in Christ, the Lamb of God, who takes away the sin of the world.

20. Answers will vary. Christ is the Word through whom all things were made (John 1:1–2), and He is the Lamb whose blood redeems men for God. Without Christ at the center, no hymn or sermon or worship can properly be called Christian.

Everything in Order (Vision)

21. The Corinthian congregation was deeply divided. Apparently, some were disrupting the services by babbling in strange tongues, and others were insisting on speaking, even to the point of interrupting others. Women, ordinarily quiet, were asking questions and commenting to the embarrassment of their husbands. In view of the "everything goes" approach to worship, the apostle lays down some simple rules. Only two or three may speak, each in turn. There is no speaking in tongues unless it can be made intelligible, and the women are to remain silent. Since God is a God of order and peace, everything conducted in His name should be done in an appropriate and orderly manner.

22. The liturgy provides an orderly framework in which the Word of God may be heard and taught, and the priestly people of God would have scope and room for their prayers and praises as one body. Since the liturgy is primarily drawn from the Scriptures, it ensures that the Word of God dwells richly among the priesthood.

23. Answers will vary. The purpose of this question is to draw people out of themselves and into the corporate nature of worship. Too often, we are concerned only with our "being fed" or what we "get out of" worship. Every priest has a purpose in the worship of the priesthood, whether to sing, to pray, or to encourage. Those priests who are called and ordained as pastors are given to preach, teach, and administer the Sacraments. One often neglected priestly act is the word *Amen*, which is often intercepted by overeager presiders. *Amen* is the priestly word of the royal priesthood. It is saying "yes" to the prayers and blessings spoken. If nothing else, every priest belongs in church to say his or her "Amen."

The Priesthood at Work

Objectives

By the power of the Holy Spirit working through God's Word, participants will (1) recognize the priesthood of their various vocations (callings), (2) see their various responsibilities in church, home, and society, and (3) approach the daily tasks of their lives as a priestly calling of God.

Opening Worship

Read Psalm 145 together. Then, sing "We Give Thee But Thine Own" (*LSB* 781; *ELH* 445; *CW* 485; *LW* 405; *LBW* 410) or "Forth in Thy Name, O Lord, I Go" (*LSB* 854; *ELH* 506; *CW* 456; *LW* 380; *LBW* 505).

Prayer: Gracious God, our heavenly Father, Your Son has called us into priestly service in the world, promising that as we do unto others, so we have done unto Him; grant that we freely and gladly bless our neighbor by our callings, and in so doing, show forth the mercy and love our Savior, Jesus Christ, in whose name we pray. Amen.

Focus

24. Answers will vary. The purpose of this question is to have each person focus on the various aspects of his or her calling as father, mother, son, daughter, employer, employee, citizen, and congregation member. In identifying our various "hats," we are also indicating the places where and the people whom we serve.

Priests in Church, Home, and Community (Inform)

25. The Church is ordered by God as those who preach and those who hear. The priesthood supports their pastor with a fair wage and support for his family as laborers worthy of their hire. Pastor should also be given the honor and obedience that befits their office as those who speak "in the stead and by the command" of Jesus Christ. Each member of the priesthood is responsible for the support of his or her pastor. Have each

person talk about the various ways members of the congregation can support their pastor in his work.

26. The home is ordered by God as husbands over wives, and parents over children. The husband is the head of the family as Christ is the head of the Church. The wife is subordinate to her husband, that is, ordered under him as the Church is ordered under Christ. Note that the word for *subordinate* is a word used in the military to indicate every person in his or her rank. The common translation of *submission* does not quite capture the nuance. The wife is not submissive to her husband but subordinate to him. He is the bishop of the household, and she is the deaconess who is there to assist him. Similarly, children are ordered under their parents and are to be obedient to them in the Lord, that is, so long as what parents command is according to God's will. Since a parent's word is God's Word for a child, parents are not to frustrate their children with too many rules, but nurture them in the instruction and discipline of the Lord. Christian parents fulfill their priesthood by bringing their children to Holy Baptism, teaching them the catechism and the Scriptures, and preparing them for Holy Communion and full adult participation in the Church.

27. The priesthood of the worker is to serve his or her boss as though serving the Lord Himself. Ephesians reminds us that Christians ought to be the best workers they can be, since they are serving Christ in their work. The priesthood of a boss is to be kind and fair to his or her workers, knowing that we all have one master who is Jesus Christ, who came to be the servant of all.

28. The priesthood of a citizen is to render obedience, honor, respect, revenue, and taxes to the governing authority as God's minister. In Lutheran theology, temporal government is sometimes called the kingdom of the left as compared to the kingdom of the right, a kingdom of grace that is manifested in the Church. The Lutheran distinction of the two kingdoms orients the Christian favorably toward the government. Lutherans do not believe in a Christian nation but in a nation in which Christians actively participate in government as their priestly vocation.

29. The Christian's priesthood also calls him or her to pray for those in authority, since prayer is uniquely priestly work. If the Christian does not intercede on behalf of the state, who will?

30. Christians are bound to obey the government as God's representative of law. However, when the government forces someone to go against the Word of God or conscience, which is the Law of God written in men's hearts (Romans 2:14–15), then, "we must obey God rather than men."

To Whom It Is Given (Connect)

31. In the episode in 1 Samuel, Saul becomes impatient when Samuel is delayed in arriving, so he offers the sacrifice himself. This is outside his vocation as king and intrudes on the vocation of Samuel whom God had authorized to make sacrifices. This is a good illustration of the nature of authority as permission granted by another. It was not given to Saul to make sacrifices, and as expedient and convenient as that act may have been, it did not please the Lord and resulted in judgment on Saul. The notion that the end justifies the means can never be used as an excuse to take up what God has not granted. For this reason, though the Lord's Supper is given to the whole Church, it is not given to all to administer it. In the case of an emergency, a layperson may administer Baptism where death appears to be imminent and no pastor is available. This is based on the principle that no one may die apart from the Gospel of Jesus Christ. Such a case is similar to a citizen's arrest in which a citizen, not authorized to enforce the law, does so to protect his neighbor and then only until the authorities arrive on the scene. At a time other than an emergency, this would constitute impersonating an officer. In this episode, Saul was impersonating a sacrificial minister.

32. Hebrews makes the strong argument that Jesus did not make Himself to be the High Priest of the world, but He was called and anointed by God the Father as is attested in the psalms quoted. If this is true of Christ, the eternal Son of God, how much more is it true of His priests? We do not baptize ourselves, but we are baptized into the priesthood by God through His minister. Likewise, God is the one who places us into our various callings and offices, which we receive as a gift from Him. For this reason, we do not speak of our rights as a priesthood but of the gift of our priesthood, since this comes from God and not from ourselves.

Priestly Perfection (Vision)

33. Sometimes people have a romantic view of the Christian life as being religious or always involved in church work. The Lutheran understanding of priesthood as a calling or vocation emphasizes that Christ can and is served in our various callings, no matter how mundane or worldly they might appear. Christian perfection is not found in some religious life removed from the world but is found in true fear of God under the Law, true faith in Christ according to the Gospel, that for His sake our sins are forgiven, and that He clothes us with His perfect righ-teousness. In that liberty, we serve God and the neighbor in our various callings. This was

the genius of the Lutheran Reformation that restored the dignity of priesthood to the various callings of people in the world.

The Office of the Holy Ministry

Objectives

By the power of the Holy Spirit working through God's Word, participants will (1) understand the concept of office as it relates to the Holy Ministry, (2) recognize that an office entails authority and responsibility, and (3) rejoice that God has established the Office of the Holy Ministry in the Church for the blessing of the priestly people of God.

Opening Worship

Read Psalm 84 together. Then, sing "Preach You the Word" (*LSB* 586; *CW* 544; *LW* 259).

Prayer: Gracious God, our heavenly Father, Your Son established the Office of the Holy Ministry by His chosen apostles so that your Church might ever hear your saving Word; we thank you for the gift of the Office of the Holy Ministry and for those who fill it. Bless all pastors of your Church that they may preach and preside in our congregations to the upbuilding of your people and to the glory of your holy name, through Jesus Christ, our Lord.

Focus

34. The purpose of this question is to stimulate a discussion about the importance of the gift of authority in everyday life.

We live under many authority structures according to the Fourth Commandment: parents, employers, government, the Church. If there were no notion of authority, there would be chaos and anarchy. When the authority structures break down or are disabled, civilized society is impossible. We recognize the need for authority, especially in the civil realm. Though we say that anyone can be president, in fact, only one person is the president. If everyone is in charge, then in fact no one is actually in charge. Knowing where the authority is and who holds it is essential for life together. It is liberating to be under authority, because then you are free to do your vocation without having to look over your shoulder at what's happening around you.

Disciples and Apostles (Inform)

35. Though all apostles were disciples, not all disciples were apostles. Jesus had a large circle of disciples that were loosely associated with Him. Included in that wider circle were the women who followed Him and attended to Him. In Jesus' day, it was unheard of for a rabbi to have female disciples. Out of that greater crowd of disciples, Jesus called twelve apostles. A disciple is one who follows and learns from His teacher. All Christians are made disciples through Baptism and teaching (Matthew 28:16–20). An apostle is one who is sent with the authority of another. Jesus here specifically authorizes them to preach the kingdom and to drive out demons. They would do precisely what Jesus was doing, "in His stead and by His command." This was a limited authorization, a kind of internship for the apostles, in which they would learn what it means to be authorized by the Son of God Himself.

36. After Jesus' death and resurrection, He met with His eleven (the Twelve minus Judas) to authorize them. Jesus has all authority in heaven and on earth, which He received from the Father. On the basis of His authority, Jesus authorizes the disciples to make disciples or to disciple the nations. The means for accomplishing this task was through Baptism in the triune name and through teaching. Jesus' mandate extended to all nations until the end of the age. Clearly, this was more than eleven men could accomplish in a lifetime. When men are called and ordained into the Office of the Holy Ministry today, their work is an extension of this original apostolic work, discipling the nations through Baptism and teaching. For this reason, the pastoral office is seen as an apostolic office, which is in continuity with the apostles Jesus sent.

37. Jesus promises that the words of His apostles are His words and are to be heard as though He Himself were speaking. The forgiveness of the apostle is the forgiveness of Christ, crucified and risen with the wounds to prove it. In the Small Catechism instruction on Confession and Absolution, Luther has the pastor ask the penitent, "Do you believe that my forgiveness is God's forgiveness?" The answer to that question hinges on our understanding of what it means to speak with the authority of another. When a called and ordained servant of Christ speaks out of Christ's office, we can be as certain of this as if a voice from heaven called out to us and spoke into our own ears. Of course, this authority to speak for Christ pertains to forgiveness of sins, not the color of the walls or the kind of carpet laid on the church floor.

38. In Romans 10, there is a progression of rhetorical questions that move from faith to hearing to preaching to having been sent to preach. Faith seeks an object. It clings to the objective Word of Christ, which was preached and heard. The preaching of the Word is objective as well.

It is not the result of a person's subjective feeling that God has called him to preach but an objective reality that God has specifically sent him to a particular place and people to proclaim the Word.

39. This episode in Acts is vitally important toward understanding the nature of the office. Judas was unfaithful and betrayed the Lord. He killed himself and left his office vacant. But the apostolic office remains even when the apostle goes bad, and that this is the beauty of the gift of office, because the office does not derive its authority from the person but the person from the office. Therefore, as our Lutheran Confessions remind us, "Both the Sacraments and Word are effective because of Christ's institution and command, even if they are administered by evil men" (*Augsburg Confession* VIII 2). The office provides an objective certainty that a person cannot. So, even if Judas forgave sins, they were forgiven by virtue of his office.

40. The key word in this passage is *some*. Some are given to be prophets, apostles, evangelists, pastors, and teachers. We aren't sure what all these titles refer to in this passage or even if these offices were in effect at the time of Paul. He might be referring to the various offices of the Word throughout the course of history. Nonetheless, it is the crucified, risen, and ascended Christ who gives these gifts to His Church so that the whole priesthood of God, that is, the whole Church, attains the unity of the faith and grows in knowledge to full maturity in Christ. As the Church is built up by Word and Sacrament, it grows together into Christ, the head of the Church, and builds itself up in love as each priest of the royal priesthood does his or her work.

41. The issue in Corinth was that people were playing favorites. Some preferred Paul, some Cephas, some Apollos. Some didn't need pastors at all and said, "I belong to Christ." Over and against this, the apostle Paul points out that he preached and Apollos watered (baptized), but it was God who gave the growth. This is one reason that pastors typically wore vestments that covered their own persons and personality. Pastors are interchangeable instruments who speak the Word of Jesus Christ, who wishes to be heard through them. As the *Apology of the Augsburg Confession* notes, "Christ requires that they [pastors and bishops] teach in such a way that He Himself is heard because He says, 'The one . . . hears Me.' Therefore, He wishes His own voice, His own Word, to be heard, not human traditions" (Ap XXVIII 19).

A Stewardship (Connect)

42. The apostle Paul calls his apostolic office a stewardship of the mysteries of God. A mystery is a hidden thing that is revealed by the Word of God. The Office of the Holy Ministry reveals these hidden

things of Christ by the preaching of the Word of Christ. Among the mysteries in the New Testament are the resurrection and change of our bodies on the last day (1 Corinthians 15:51), the uniting of all things under Christ (Ephesians 1:9–10), Christ Himself (Colossians 2:2), the incarnation and reign of Christ (1 Timothy 3:16). One might also include the Sacraments as *mysteries*, which was the earliest term for the Sacraments in Greek. (*Sacrament* is a borrowed term in Latin.) Your rebirth in Baptism is a mystery, something hidden from sight that must be revealed by the Word, as are the body and blood of Christ in the Lord's Supper. The Office of the Holy Ministry is Christ's authorized steward of these mysteries, dispensing the gifts of Christ to His royal priesthood as a household steward sees to it that all the servants receive their fair share (Luke 12:42).

43. The Lord's Supper, Holy Baptism, and Holy Absolution were all entrusted to the inner core of apostles who were the first pastors of the Church. This does not mean that the Sacraments belong to the clergy as a private possession. Rather, the Word and Sacraments are entrusted to the whole Church in the Office of the Holy Ministry, which also belongs to the whole Church, so that these things might go on in the stead and by the command of Christ. The Office of the Holy Ministry is authorized to preach the Gospel and administer the Sacraments for the blessing and benefit of the whole Church.

Accountability (Vision)

44. Paul uses the image of a builder. One lays the foundation, and another builds on it. Pastoral work is always building on what came before. Paul indicates that a pastor's work will be judged most severely by the Lord, since it is the Lord's office. If the builder builds with cheap materials, the structure will not withstand the fire of testing. If he builds with good materials, the structure will endure. This is a call for pastors to preach the Word as Law and Gospel and not their own pious opinions. Notice that though the work of the builder is judged, the builder is not judged by his work. He will be saved, though the one who builds shoddily will suffer loss. This is why a pastor's concerns may not be the same as his congregation's or church body's leadership. His concern is faithfulness to the Gospel of Jesus Christ, over and against any institutional concerns, for he is accountable to God for the kind of material he uses to build.

45. This passage is important from a number of aspects. The elders of Ephesus are also called overseers (bishops) and shepherds (pastors). At this time, these three terms were interchangeable. We don't know how the elders of Ephesus were called or placed into office. We do know that

the Holy Spirit was the one who made them overseers, and it is to God Himself that they and Paul were finally accountable. The Church is God's flock, purchased with the holy, precious blood and innocent suffering and death of Jesus Christ. The Office of the Holy Ministry is called to care for God's treasured possession—His royal and holy priesthood.

46. Hebrews and James both underscore the accountability of the office. Pastors must give an account of their stewardship. For this reason, the priesthood desires to support and obey its pastors, unless of course, they teach contrary to the Word of God. Again, as with all other authority structures, "We must obey God rather than men" (Acts 5:29). Answers will vary as to the best way to handle such unfortunate situations. Respect and honor for the office must be maintained at all times, even when those who hold it are less than honorable. Usually, church bodies are able to supply outside pastors and counselors who can help address a situation in which a pastor is teaching false doctrine. Every Christian is called, by virtue of his or her priesthood, to be a discerning hearer of God's Word and to respectfully hold pastors accountable for their teaching and practice.

Qualities and Tasks

Objectives

By the power of the Holy Spirit working through God's Word, participants will (1) learn the biblical qualities and character of candidates to the Office of the Holy Ministry, (2) recognize what are the essential tasks of the office, (3) see his or her own priesthood as a means to assist and free the pastor to do the proper work of the Holy Ministry.

Opening Worship

Read Psalm 119:1–8 together. Then, sing "Speak, O Lord, Your Servant Listens" (*LSB* 589; *ELH* 230; *CW* 283; *LW* 339; *TLH* 296).

Prayer: Holy and most gracious God, Your Son chose men to be His apostles and sent them with authority to preach and preside in His name. Send also capable and qualified men in our day to shepherd Your people, and raise up among us those who will preach Your Word with courage and administer your gifts faithfully, that we might be strengthened in our priesthood to serve and praise You, through Jesus Christ, our Lord.

Focus

47. Everyone has expectations, even of their pastors. This question is designed to explore what those expectations are. Opinions will vary widely. The important thing is that they are discussed along with people's perceptions of what the essential tasks of the pastoral office are.

A Noble Task (Inform)

48. The apostle Paul lists a variety of qualities and characteristics of the man who desires the office of overseer in the Christian congregation. Among them, he must be the husband of only one wife, be a good father, manage his household, be temperate, disciplined, respectable, hospitable, able to teach and refute false teaching, be gentle, sober, and neither quarrelsome nor greedy. The overall picture is of a man with a sound reputation both inside and outside the Church. This is essential, since scandals in the pastoral office can cause people to doubt the Word or drift away from the Church. The apostle Paul recognized that pastoral work puts a

man on the front lines against the devil's schemes, where the slightest weakness of character can give opportunity for the evil one to work his wiles.

49. Women are excluded from holding pastoral authority according to 1 Timothy 2:12. This is not to suggest that women are inferior to men, only that it is not God's will that they serve in this capacity. The apostle Paul cites the deception of Eve as her unique part in the fall, but he counterbalances it with a reference to woman's unique place in the incarnation (the bearing of the child). In 1 Corinthians 14, Paul addresses a similar issue in Corinth, where the women of the congregation were speaking in the presence of their husbands. Paul enjoins them to be silent, citing four reasons: (1) it is the common practice in all the churches; (2) it is written in the Torah that they are subordinate; (3) it is a shame for them to speak in the presence of their husbands, thereby dishonoring them; (4) it is the Lord's command. While people vigorously debate the applicability of these verses in the Church today, an important underlying fact needs to be acknowledged. Male and female are each unique and not interchangeable with each other. The unique giftedness of male and female has implications for the way each fulfills his or her priesthood in a way that honors God. The key question to be asked is not "What are my rights?" but "What honors Christ and His Word?" To this end, the Church historically has not ordained women to the Office of the Holy Ministry but has created many avenues of priestly service for women such as deaconess, teacher, and the like.

50. The Holy Scriptures are foundational for the work of the Holy Ministry. The Office of the Holy Ministry is apostolic in three senses: (1) it is sent by God; (2) it is a continuation of the ministry of the apostles; (3) it teaches the doctrine of the apostles as recorded in the Scriptures. Paul charges young pastor Timothy to attend to the public reading of the Scriptures (reading also included preaching) and reminded him that the Scriptures, as the very breath of God, were useful for doctrine, rebuke, correction, and training in righteousness so he might be fully equipped for his work. For this reason, it is essential for the pastor to be the chief student of the Scriptures, and to have ample time for the deep study of God's Word above and beyond the usual tasks of sermon preparation and Bible study.

51. Paul uses the image of a craftsman, a workman whose work meets a high level of craftsmanship and of which he need not be ashamed. To correctly handle the Word of truth means to interpret it accurately and to apply it in a way that properly distinguishes the Law and the Gospel. The Law must be preached lawfully, especially to those who are unaware or unrepentant of their sins. The Gospel must be preached evangelically without compromise or conditions. The preacher of the

Word must be willing to preach in season and out of season, when the Word is producing much fruit and also when there is little or no fruit on the congregational vine. One of the greatest challenges for a preacher, especially one who is young and inexperienced, is not to let the frustrations of parish life creep into the pulpit. Regardless of what happened at the last council meeting, the preacher is called to correct, rebuke, and encourage with patience and careful instruction using nothing other than the Word of God.

52. The apostle states that elders (presbyters or pastors) who govern the affairs of the congregation are worthy of double pay for their efforts, especially considering that they are also involved in preaching and teaching. The additional time and energy needed to administer the temporal affairs of a congregation would preclude any other income source. Recall that Paul himself worked at times in order not to be a financial burden on the young congregations he was gathering. The apostle Paul is also very careful that proper procedure be followed if a charge is made against a pastor. It must be substantiated by two or three witnesses, which was the legal standard in Judaism (see Matthew 18:18). Those who are found guilty are to be rebuked publicly, since a public office requires a public rebuke. Like any public office, pastors are visible examples for those under them.

53. False doctrine is a cancer that eats away at the life of the Church. It stirs up controversies and divisions along with endless quarrels over words that wind up in envy, strife, harsh words, evil suspicions, and continual animosity and friction. Paul knew of such things in his own day and warned Timothy that things would not get better as the time of the end drew near. Another cancer that eats away at the Church is greed and financial corruption. Paul warns that some see godliness as an opportunity to profit, and he knew nothing of the television and the lucrative publishing industry we have today. His warning applies to pastor and priesthood alike: the love of money is the root of all sorts of evil. Money itself is not evil; it is a gift from God. But the love of money turns the good gift into an idol that consumes.

The Lord Is My Pastor (Connect)

54. Of course, Psalm 23 is about the Lord. David, the shepherd-king, writes a sheep's-eye view of what it is like to have the Lord as His shepherd. In Latin, the word for shepherd is *pastores,* from which we get the word *pastor.* A pastor is a shepherd of a flock. Psalm 23 can be read as a kind of job description of the good pastor. His flock lacks nothing. He makes them rest in the green pastures of God's Word; he leads them to the quiet, restful waters of their Baptism, and he restores their soul,

picking them up when they fall. He guides his congregation in the well-worn ruts of righteousness that are the way of Jesus' dying and rising. He walks with them through the dark valley as they face their own death. He brings them the comfort of the Word—the rod of the Law, the staff of the Gospel. He prepares a rich table, the body and blood of the Good Shepherd, in the presence of the enemy—sin, death, the devil. He anoints the head of each of his flock with the healing balm of forgiveness. Their cup overflows, so that goodness and mercy follow them all the days of their lives in the confidence that they will dwell with God forever. This would be a suitable job description for a good pastor.

55. In the fifth chapter of 1 Peter, Peter addresses the elders (pastors) and exhorts them to be shepherds to the flocks entrusted to their care, watching over the priesthood willingly and eagerly. They are not to use their position to lord it over their people but to lead them by example. That's the curious thing about sheep. They only respond to being led. They can't be driven like cattle. Pastors are not ranchers, driving their people, nor are they executives, managing their people. They are humble shepherds serving under the chief shepherd and bishop, Jesus Christ. His promise is a crown of life that won't fade away, awaiting all who trust in Him. The goal of pastoral work is not success but faith and faithfulness.

Preaching and Prayer (Vision)

56. The Greek widows were being neglected in the distribution of food. This could have turned into a divisive thing for the first congregation of Christians, since animosity between Hebraic and Greek people was strong. The twelve apostles wisely gathered the whole company of disciples together. (Note the distinction of apostle and disciple in this passage.) They advised them to choose seven godly men from among them. Having done so, the congregation presented these seven men to the apostles who ordained them into their office with prayer and the laying on of hands. Though the passage does not refer to these seven as deacons, it refers to their works as a "service (*diakonia*) of tables." The apostles wisely focused on the essence of their office, namely "the service of the Word of God and prayer." The Augsburg Confession states that the essential authority of the Office of the Holy Ministry is "to preach the Gospel, to forgive and retain sins, and to administer Sacraments" (*Augsburg Confession* XXVIII 5)

57. Recognizing the essence of the Office of the Holy Ministry as preaching the Word and administering the Sacraments, the congregation as a priesthood has the opportunity to free its pastor to do his proper work and to open up new possibilities through outreach and works of

service in the community. The potential distractions to the ministry of Word and Sacrament are many and varied, from congregational issues to personal crises to synodical and church body politics. While these may be important, they are not essential. The pastor and the baptized priesthood can work together to ensure that the Office of the Holy Ministry is able to run unencumbered so that the Word may be preached, the Sacraments administered and distributed, and the priesthood would have ample opportunity for prayer.

Call and Ordination

Objectives

By the power of the Holy Spirit working through God's Word, participants will (1) learn how pastors are chosen and placed into office, (2) understand the significance of the custom of laying on of hands, and (3) appreciate the gift of ordination.

Opening Worship

Read Psalm 92 together. Then sing "God of the Prophets, Bless the Prophets' Sons" (*LSB* 682; *ELH* 501; *CW* 543; *LW* 258; *TLH* 483).

Prayer: Holy and most gracious God, our Father in heaven, stir up Your Holy Spirit in Your holy Church and fan into flame the gifts of Your holy office. Grant that those who preach Your Word would do so with power and conviction and that those who hear would be edified and strengthened in their faith in Christ. Send faithful shepherds to Your congregations, remember those who are seeking pastors, and raise up among us a generation of faithful men who will preach and preside in season and out of season; through Jesus Christ, our Lord, who lives and reigns with You and the Holy Spirit, one God, now and forever. Amen.

Focus

58. We have a variety of mechanisms for choosing people for public office. In America, this is most often done by democratic election. Sometimes, officials are appointed and their appointment ratified. We also have mechanisms for placing people into public office. These ceremonies may be simple or quite elaborate, as in the inauguration of a president. There is a specified rite for inaugurating a president that includes a solemn vow, made with a hand on the Bible, to defend the constitution of the United States. We can be certain that people belong in office as they have been lawfully chosen and installed. In fact, the chief purpose of an inauguration ceremony is to make public the fact that this person is now assuming the office to which he or she has been elected. The Office of the Holy Ministry is a public office in the Church and is treated in a similar fashion. Men are chosen to serve by call and are ordained to office.

Chosen to Serve (Inform)

59. When faced with the vacancy left by Judas, the apostles chose two men who had been with them the entire time from John's Baptism to Jesus' resurrection and who were eyewitnesses to Jesus' resurrection. They then commended the matter to God in prayer and drew lots. While this episode is descriptive of what was done and not prescriptive of what must be done, it is nevertheless enlightening and instructive. The apostles used the best reasoned judgment to arrive at a short list of candidates and then left the final decision to the Lord. However, the Church chooses and places its candidates for the Office of the Holy Ministry, and the procedure should reflect the fact that it is God who calls through the various mechanisms of the congregation, not the congregation by itself.

60. The congregation of disciples picked the seven men who were to serve, and the apostles prayed over them with the laying on of hands.

61. In the Books of Acts, 1 Timothy, and Titus, it appears that elders (pastors) were appointed. Paul and Barnabas appointed elders in all the cities where congregations had been gathered. Paul instructs Timothy and Titus to select suitable men to be elders and overseers and gives the criteria for their selection.

62. While the right and authority to call and ordain lies with every gathering of the priesthood, it does not follow that each congregation may or should act autonomously. When the Treatise was written, bishops were refusing to ordain pastors to Evangelical (Lutheran) congregations. Faced with the prospects of no pastors, the Lutheran reformers reasoned that the Church as the royal priesthood may never be denied pastors. So, when the existing structures refuse to provide pastors, the priesthood must, for the sake of the Gospel, take matters into its own hands. However a man is selected, whether by a congregational vote or by a committee or by appointment, the method and means should reflect God's activity. A congregation acting alone may call someone who will confirm them in their error and scratch their itching ears, as Paul said. Outside counsel helps to guard against this. A bishop appointing a pastor may have his own interests in mind and not those of a congregation. Historically, no pastor was ever forced on a congregation but was always called with its consent.

63. The Holy Spirit made the elders of Ephesus overseers of God's flock. The tendency on our part is to concern ourselves with how something is done more than over what is being done. While the process of calling a pastor may seem tinged by special interests and politics or some people may not be happy with the particular choice, it is helpful to remember that it is God who calls the man in, with, and under the machinery of the call.

64. This question is intended for open discussion. Certainly, employing the Word of God and prayer in all facets of the call process helps to underscore God's hidden hand in this matter. Further, the involvement of neighboring pastors helps to emphasize the catholicity of the pastoral office, that this is not simply an isolated congregation, but one in fellowship with other congregations who also recognize the Office of the Holy Ministry in that place.

With the Laying on of Hands (Connect)

65. The apostles laid their hands on the men with their prayers. The laying on of hands was a custom inherited from the Old Testament. Moses laid his hands on the Joshua, his successor, and so Joshua received the "spirit of wisdom" that Moses had (Deuteronomy 34:9). This is not to suggest that power is transmitted mechanically through a succession of hands laid on heads. The laying on of hands was a sign of specificity, indicating that a particular person was involved whether for prayer, healing, or placing into office. Hands were laid on the Old Testament sacrifices prior to slaughter. Jesus laid hands on the sick and demonized for healing and on the little children for blessing. The practice of installing into office with the laying on of hands likely came from the synagogue and the ordination of a rabbi.

66. Paul and the company of elders laid hands on Timothy at his ordination. Paul refers to a gift that was given through a prophetic utterance (1 Timothy 4:14) and a gift of God that was given through the laying on of hands. While it is not clear what exactly those gifts were, it is clear that Timothy was gifted for the office into which he was placed. The gifts pertaining to the Office of the Holy Ministry do not inhere to the pastor but to the pastoral office. Since the Office of the Holy Ministry is an office of the Word, as the pastor is a servant of the Word, it stands to reason that this office would come with the requisite gifts to fulfill the duties of the office. The laying on of hands indicates that Timothy specifically has been chosen by God to occupy the office, and this is being publicly ratified and confirmed by the Word of God and prayer.

Ordained (Vision)

67. Timothy did not take his position on his own initiative or by his own scheming; it was given to him as a gift. This provided him confidence in his work. Timothy was quite young in a culture that valued the wisdom of age and looked down upon the young as ignorant and inexperienced. He would be challenged by older men as well as the lusts of

youth. New and complex heresies were on the horizon that would test his doctrinal acumen. The fact that his office came with the promises of God's blessing and the gifts of the Spirit would certainly bring comfort to Timothy, and to any pastor, in times of doubt and despair.

68. From ancient times in the Church, ordination was assigned to the bishops or overseers. Our Lutheran Confessions acknowledge this but point out that this is by human, not divine, arrangement (*The Power and the Primacy of the Pope* 63–67). Though the congregation may have a direct role in calling its pastor, it nevertheless receives its pastor as a gift through the ordination of fellow pastors. This outside-of-ourselves character of ordination serves to underscore that these are gifts of Christ, who sits enthroned at the right hand of God as the head of the Church.

In summary, the holy priesthood of the baptized and the Office of the Holy Ministry are not two competing entities or two classes of Christian. To serve in the Office of the Holy Ministry is a priestly calling like every other vocation. Priesthood is our baptismal dignity before God whereby our lives are made living sacrifices through the one atoning sacrifice of Jesus Christ. The Office of the Holy Ministry is the office that serves the priesthood with the gifts of Word and Sacrament, enabling and enlivening them to live in the fear of God, faith in Christ, and service of love to the neighbor.

Appendix of Lutheran Teaching

Below, you will find examples of how the first Lutherans addressed the issues of priesthood and ministry. They will help you understand the Lutheran difference.

The Augsburg Confession (1530)

Because the nature of the Office of the Holy Ministry was a point of contention between Lutherans and the papacy, the Augsburg Confession and its Apology have much to say concerning it. Unlike the radical reformers who made every Christian a minister, the Lutherans retained the Office of the Holy Ministry as God's institution, but they did not elevate the pastor as office holder above that of any other baptized Christian. Every Christian was a priest to God within the priesthood of Jesus Christ, and certain baptized priests were called and ordained to be pastors. Furthermore, the Lutheran doctrine of the two kingdoms restricted pastoral authority to the authority to preach the Word and administer the Sacraments. Temporal authority was outside the scope of the Office of the Holy Ministry.

Article V—The Ministry

So that we may obtain this faith, the ministry of teaching the Gospel and administering the Sacraments was instituted. Through the Word and Sacraments, as through instruments, the Holy Spirit is given [John 20:22]. He works faith, when and where it pleases God [John 3:8], in those who hear the good news that God justifies those who believe that they are received into grace for Christ's sake. This happens not through our own merits, but for Christ's sake. Our churches condemn the Anabaptists and others who think that through their own preparations and works the Holy Spirit comes to them without the external Word.

Article XIV—Order in the Church

Our churches teach that no one should publicly teach in the Church, or administer the Sacraments, without a rightly ordered call.

Article XXVII 5–12—Church Authority

Many entered monastic life through ignorance. They were not able to judge their own strength, though they were old enough. They were trapped and compelled to remain, even though some could have been freed by the kind provision of canon law. This was more the case in convents of women than of monks, although more consideration should have been shown the weaker sex (1 Peter 3:7). This rigor displeased many good people before this time, who saw that young men and women were thrown into convents for a living. They saw what unfortunate results came of this procedure, how it created scandals, and what snares were cast upon consciences! They were sad that the authority of canon law in so great a matter was utterly set aside and despised. In addition to all these evil things, a view of vows was added that displeased even the more considerate monks. They taught that monastic vows were equal to Baptism. They taught that a monastic life merited forgiveness of sins and justification before God. Yes, they even added that the monastic life not only merited righteousness before God, but even greater merit, since it was said that the monastic life not only kept God's basic law, but also the so-called "evangelical counsels."

Apology of the Augsburg Confession

Philip Melanchthon also wrote an Apology, or defense, of the Augsburg Confession to further demonstrate, this time at greater length, the soundness of Lutheran beliefs and practices. Like the Augsburg Confession, the Apology remains a standard of Lutheran teaching.

Article XIII 7–13—The Number and Use of the Sacraments

The adversaries understand *priesthood* not about the ministry of the Word, and giving out the Sacraments to others, but as referring to sacrifice. This is as though there should be a priesthood like the Levitical one [Leviticus 8–9] to sacrifice for the people and merit the forgiveness of sins for others in the New Testament. We teach that the sacrifice of Christ dying on the cross has been enough for the sins of the whole world. There is no need for other sacrifices, as though Christ's sacrifice were not enough for our sins. So people are justified not because of any other sacrifices, but because of this one sacrifice of Christ, if they believe that they have been redeemed by this sacrifice. So they are called priests, not in order to make any sacrifices for the people as in the Law, that by these they may merit forgiveness of sins for the people. Rather, they are called to teach the Gospel and administer the Sacraments to the people. Nor do we have another priesthood like the Levitical, as the Epistle to the

Hebrews teaches well enough [Hebrews 8]. But if ordination is understood as carrying out the ministry of the Word, we are willing to call ordination a Sacrament. For the ministry of the Word has God's command and has glorious promises, "The gospel . . . is the power of God for salvation to everyone who believes" (Romans 1:16). Likewise, "So shall My word be that goes out from My mouth; it shall not return to Me empty, but it shall accomplish that which I purpose" (Isaiah 55:11). If ordination is understood in this way, neither will we refuse to call the laying on of hands a Sacrament. For the Church has the command to appoint ministers, which should be most pleasing to us, because we know that God approves this ministry and is present in the ministry. It is helpful, so far as can be done, to honor the ministry of the Word with every kind of praise against fanatical people. These fanatics imagine that the Holy Spirit is given not through the Word, but through certain preparations of their own. For example, they imagine He is given if they sit unoccupied and silent in far-off places, waiting for illumination, as the Enthusiasts formerly taught and the Anabaptists now teach.

Power and Primacy of the Pope

The Treatise on the Power and Primacy of the Pope was written by Philip Melanchthon in 1540 as a follow-up to the Augsburg Confession and the Apology, which had also been authored by Melanchthon. In two sections, he treats the false claims made by the papacy concerning the rights of the Roman bishop and the genuine authority that bishops, or pastors, have under the Gospel.

65–70

Since the grades of bishop and pastor are not different by divine authority, it is clear that ordination administered by a pastor in his own church is valid by divine law. Therefore, when the regular bishops become enemies of the Church or are unwilling to administer ordination, the churches retain their own right [to ordain their own ministers]. Wherever the Church is, there is the authority to administer the Gospel. Therefore, it is necessary for the Church to retain the authority to call, elect, and ordain ministers. This authority is a gift that in reality is given to the Church. No human power can take this gift away from the Church. As Paul testifies to the Ephesians, when "He ascended . . . He gave gifts to men" (Ephesians [4:8]). He lists among the gifts specifically belonging to the Church "pastors and teachers" [4:11], and adds that they are given for the ministry, "for building up the body of Christ" [4:12]. So wherever there is a True Church, the right to elect and ordain ministers necessarily exists. In the same way, in a case of necessity even a layman absolves and becomes the minister and pastor of another. Augustine tells the story of two Christians in a ship, one of whom baptized the catechumen, who after Baptism then absolved the baptizer. Here belong the statements of Christ that testify that the Keys have been given to the Church, and not merely to certain persons, "Where two or three are gathered in My name . . ." [Matthew 18:20]. Finally, Peter's statement also confirms this, "You are . . . a royal priesthood" [1 Peter 2:9]. These words apply to the True Church, which certainly has the right to elect and ordain ministers, since it alone has the priesthood. A most common custom of the Church also testifies to this. Formerly, the people elected pastors and bishops [Acts 14:23]. Then came a bishop, either of that church or a neighboring one, who confirmed the one elected by the laying on of hands [1 Timothy 4:14]. Ordination was nothing else than such a ratification.

Glossary

bishop. In the Scriptures, this term (Greek: *episkopos*) is used synonymously with *elder* (Greek: *presbyteros*) and *shepherd* and *pastor*. From the second century, it referred to a pastor who supervised other pastors in a given region.

call. The mechanism whereby a man is chosen for a specific area of pastoral work. The call specifies who, what, and where.

deacon. Traditionally, an assistant to a bishop or overseer (see Philippians 1:1). The traditional work of a deacon was to assist in the Divine Service and to care for the poor and needy. Deacons also brought Holy Communion to the shut-ins.

elder. Also presbyter. In the Scriptures, this term is synonymous with overseer (bishop) or shepherd (pastor). From the second century, the office of elder (presbyter) was a lesser order of clergy under the bishop, corresponding roughly to a parish pastor today. This distinction was by human arrangement.

ministry. Used in both a wide and narrow sense. In the wide sense, any area of service; in the narrow sense, the Office of the Holy Ministry.

office. A specific authority entrusted to specifically chosen people to do specific functions. For example, the Office of the Holy Ministry is the authority to preach, teach, and administer the Sacraments.

ordination. The ratification or confirmation of the call through prayer, the Word of God, and the laying on of hands. Ordination formally and publicly places a person in office.

presbyter. See elder.

priest. In the Old Testament, a Levitical minister of the tabernacle or temple who offered sacrifices on behalf of Israel. In the New Testament, any baptized believer in Christ. Luther and the reformers frequently used the word *priest* to refer to pastors, following medieval usage. This sometimes creates confusion when reading Luther or the Lutheran Confessions.

priesthood. An order of priests. Priests are never isolated as individuals.

vocation. Also a calling. Refers to one's position in life in terms of where God has placed him or her and how He has gifted that individual.